CONFIDENT FACE

Embracing your Authentic Beauty

Esther Jacob

CONFIDENT FACE
Embracing your Authentic Beauty

Copyright © 2021 by Esther Jacob

Unless otherwise indicated, scripture quotations are taken from the Holy Bible in several versions including the New International Version (NIV) and New Living Translation (NLT).

Confident Face

Paperback ISBN Number: 978-1-9160600-9-8
Hardback ISBN Number: 978-1-8384576-1-7
e-Book ISBN Number: 978-1-8384576-2-4

Published by Authentic Worth
Website: www.authenticworth.com

Manuscript Submissions
Email: submissions@authenticworth.com

Disclaimer

This book is not a step-by-step guide on how to get rid of spots, hyperpigmentation, blackheads, acne or any type of skin condition. The products used by the author can be purchased at your own discretion. Recommendations are based on what the author currently uses or has used in the past. If you would like to know how to get rid of spots, blackheads, acne, or any type of skin issue, consult a professional dermatologist or visit your local GP.

Confident Face

Acknowledgments

Honouring those who constantly add value in your life shouldn't be taken for granted. My first vote of thanks is to my Father, for His consistent strength and support in helping me to write this book project. Writing is a rich gift and will continue using it to inspire and influence the lives of others. Thank you to my family, my friends and loved ones. *Keeley Stephenson*; a beautiful and precious sister who wrote the Foreword of this book, and a special thanks to two ladies; *Wendi Odili* and *Melvina E* for their contributions towards this book project in sharing experiences about their skincare journey.

OTHER BOOKS WRITTEN BY ESTHER JACOB:

It's Time to Heal – *A woman's journey to self-discovery and freedom.*

Completion – *From the perspective of brokenness.*

From Glory to Glory – *Great beauty in seasons of pain; Strong at the broken places.*

The Power of a Forward-Thinking Mindset – *Breaking strongholds in the mind.*

Confident Face – *Embracing your authentic beauty.*

All books can be found on **www.authenticworth.com/books**

Praise for Authentic Worth

Authentic Worth is a movement purposeful about making the world of publishing more accessible to every-day writers and hopeful authors of all backgrounds. The workshops run by the Founder, Esther Jacob, are passionate, thoroughly researched and well delivered. I am excited and hopeful about the future impact of this platform – **Anu Adebogun.**

I love what Authentic Worth does and all they are doing to help upcoming authors/writers. It is definitely needed in this generation. It is great to know that there is such a company helping people who would otherwise have no idea where to start, literally walking with them along the journey. I have attended one of Authentic Worth's events which was very insightful and it was amazing recently seeing a new author emerging through the help of Authentic Worth. I look forward to attending another event by the company in the future and would definitely recommend – **Maria Tayo.**

An extremely helpful range of services offered with the utmost professionalism. I highly recommend Authentic Worth for budding authors – **Sarah Adebambo.**

Confident Face

Authentic Worth is an amazing platform. I had the privilege of meeting the Founder and she is such a lovely lady. So gentle, approachable and dedicated to supporting others. Will definitely recommend this platform to anyone looking to publish a book. You will not be disappointed! – **Pamela Nkansah.**

Authentic Worth has helped me in many ways spiritually and mentally. The company is passionate about helping and motivating others towards where they need to be, but also by focusing on yourself and what you need to improve on. Esther hosts very professional workshops which suit all different types of people and backgrounds and her books are amazing too. Thank you for all that you've done and continuing to do! – **Olivia Palmer Creigg.**

Confident Face

Contents Page

Confident Face

Foreword by Keeley Stephenson

First and foremost, I would like to congratulate my dear sister on her skincare journey and for writing such a well-needed book for our community. I've had the privilege and honour to witness many high and low moments with this amazing beauty of a woman, particularly in areas where it came to her skin.

May I add that I admire your confidence and grace, as well as the journey that it has taken you to get here. Battling with my fair share of skin struggles, I know firsthand how this feels, as well as the crushed low self-confidence that this can invite.

Esther, I just want to say that I am ever so proud of you; this may sound cliché, but your beauty supersedes any insecurity you may have had as a result of your skin, and I look forward to seeing the lives that will be changed as a result of reading your book.

You are truly wonderful and I have learned much from you, especially in the areas of confidence and becoming bolder in who I am. Your confidence will truly be the keys to break the chains of another's insecurity, and I pray that God will continue to provide you with the strength and favour to keep going on this amazing journey.

1

Confident Face

To anyone reading this, that is battling with a skin condition of any sort, I want you to know that you are beautiful; there is not a blemish, a scar, a dry blotch or spot mark that could take this away. You are beautiful just as you are. I want you to truly know this.

May you allow Esther's story to minister to your hearts as she shows you both the practical and spiritual steps she took to acquire her CONFIDENT FACE. With love, from yours truly, Keeley.

Confident Face

Introduction

At some point in our lives, there will come a time where we focus on our physical appearance, our body structure, the completion of our skin and many external attributes, whilst our mindsets are suffering from secret comparison and low self-esteem. *Note to self*: you shouldn't neglect the greatest gift which is your *mind*. Being intentional with your thought-patterns will produce growth and impact your life in many positive ways.

In my early 20s, my skin was affected by severe spots and uncontrollable blackheads. The insecurities led me to cover up my spots with foundation and powder, but to no avail. Let's say they aren't insecurities now, but I am very thankful to God that I've been able to overcome them. There were times I wanted to give up on my skin routine and the constant frustration in dealing with the unreliability of my skin reacting to different products.

To some people, you are beautiful; to other people, you aren't beautiful. **What are <u>you</u> saying about yourself?** The number of products you use will never equate to the beauty that starts within. Don't force yourself to look a certain way or become what others want you to be.

Confident Face

Understand the value of being YOU and embrace your own unique journey. What you see on social media isn't always what it looks like. Let every insecurity and flaw subside, and don't magnify your thoughts by dwelling on the past. You must understand that your pain is only for a season, and doesn't define who you are. Embrace your flaws; embrace your own journey.

My purpose for *Confident Face* is to be a blessing not only to you, but to someone you know that is currently going through internal battles affecting their physical appearance and mental health. From me to you; you are ALREADY confident! It is embedded in you. May I remind you; this book does not only focus on the physical, but working on character-building, personal development and having consistent self-control.

Confidence isn't always about being loud. *You can have private victory too*. I tend to hear comments such as: 'Esther, you are so confident!' but not realising the discipline it takes to build the confidence, especially behind closed doors when no one is looking. The most important lesson I've learnt and still continuing to learn is that *confidence never ends* when you have God dwelling within you.

It is still an on-going process that teaches us to work on ourselves daily, become better and be expectant for a great future. Confidence doesn't end when we achieve the goals set out for us; confidence is using the strengths we have to inspire others to do the same. A confident individual does not have the time to manipulate anyone. Their hearts are available to restore, replenish and bring peace in the lives of others.

Psalm 139:14 says "You are fearfully and wonderfully made." Let this be your daily reminder as you continue the journey of building confidence. Without further ado, let's get started with the first chapter...

1

○

Skin Skin Skin

Your mind must continually be renewed for your skin to flourish.

Skin skin skin…where do I start? It's been an intense journey! I remember the embarrassment and fear I experienced when going through drastic breakouts in my early 20s. To write a book about my journey on skincare takes a lot of courage. I know it isn't easy or comfortable talking about insecurities, but you know what I've come to realise? You learn to grow with it and accept yourself for who you are. If you are not confident in your flaws privately, you won't be confident in a public crowd. Let me take you on a journey…

I want you to close your eyes and think about the number of times you've experienced unexpected breakouts. Literally! Now, meditate, focus, and be still for a few seconds. Open your eyes and write down how many times you've experienced it: _____

Confident Face

The next step is: go to the bathroom and splash your face with cold water <u>without</u> using a facial towel. Let your face dry by itself. Within 10 minutes, see how your skin reacts and write whether your skin feels:

1) Dry
2) Normal
3) Oily
4) Sensitive

What is your answer? _____

Each time I wash my face without wiping it with a facial towel or applying a moisturiser, my skin becomes dry, tighter and difficult to move around, particularly my cheeks. Everyone has different issues with their skin, but what matters is how you nurture and look after it. Now, I am not an expert in skincare or the different types and what they consist of, although, I endeavour to make sure I educate those who have experienced or still are experiencing skincare issues.

I remember in my second year of university when I broke out due to the synthetic hair I purchased from a hair shop in London. The curls agreed with my face, but the quality of the hair made my skin react severely. Who remembers Premium 2 and Premium Plus hair? If you know, you know! I remember purchasing my first Brazilian hair and was excited, especially because it was around my 21st birthday and wanted to look cute! In literally less than four weeks, what did I notice? Intense breakouts on my face!

Due to the amount spent on the Brazilian hair, I wanted to make sure it lasted very well. When I purchased the 12-inch lace closure and installed it with the rest of the bundles, it came out looking good. However, why did I eventually see a small hole in the middle of the parting? I was not impressed at all. I covered the closure with the remaining hair I had left. In my mind, I told myself: "Esther, you've got this! You didn't invest to lose!"

I was determined to make sure I had it all together and not leave the house until that hole was covered. I didn't realise that same hair eventually had an impact on my skin and became addicted to breaking me out. At the time I went through this, my mind was thinking about the number of products to use in eliminating the breakouts. Through this experience, it taught me not to purchase too many products at once, and up till now, it is a key lesson applied every time I notice various products being advertised on social media.

When one spot went, another one came. I didn't know what to do and it felt as if I was in a state of laughter, confusion and tears all at the same time. One of the reasons I am sharing this is because I know how it feels to have spots, blemishes and still not feel confident.

***

IMPORTANT: Looking after your skin is very essential.

***

The most amazing factor about skin is where you've cut yourself, and eventually the skin starts to create a scab, protecting the cut from spreading further. As long as you are able to look after your skin, your skin will look after you. Think of it this way; when you pick the scab from your skin, it will attract bacteria which affects the good cells. It may feel comfortable picking off the scab, perhaps, it is a dry scab and doesn't require that much pain, but eventually, the area where the skin has been picked becomes darker, making it take a longer period of time to heal.

When our skin is not treated with intentional care, it's prone not only to the environment you surround yourself in, but the food you consume as well. Are you a healthy eater or a binge eater? Perhaps you've finished from a long day of work; you may be eager to purchase a quick takeaway from your local area because cooking would be a long task when you get home. I've been there so I can relate!

Confident Face

According to the mayoclinic.org website, it states that the following food products are advisable to improve the quality of your skin. Let's take a look:

- Fruits and vegetables
- Spinach
- Tomatoes
- Berries
- Beans, peas and lentils
- Salmon and mackerel
- Nuts

Throughout the day, I enjoy eating vegetables and fruit alongside balancing them with a few carbs. Nonetheless, one must consider their dietary habits and see what works best for them. It is important to know what foods are suited for your immune system. You may know someone who enjoys eating pizza for breakfast. For me, this would be heavy as a first meal. Or, how about hot wings and chips? ***Morleys; yummy!*** Yes, it is yummy, however, they are deep-fried and isn't always best for the outcome of your skin and overall health.

Another contributing factor to be aware of is when your neck shows signs of small spots or blackheads, as it is an indication of it spreading towards your face, cheeks, chin and forehead. I didn't realise this until I looked at my pictures;

that was when I noticed and started taking action. Perhaps my food eating habits at the time were not healthy, so that added to the breakout. It is important to ensure that what we consume is not only good for our bodies, but how we treat and nurture our skin. You must take responsibility to look after every part of your skin, ensuring that it is moisturised including your toes, back, elbows and knees.

Depending on how your skin works, if it becomes dry during winter periods, do research on products, oils and serums that will suit your skin as the winter season can be quite harsh. I am aware that our skin changes from time to time, which is why I mentioned previously that eating habits have to be in alignment to what our bodies can handle.

I remember doing a 21 Days Daniel Fast. It wasn't easy at first because my body sensed my eating habits were changing. I'd have brown rice with mixed vegetables, parsnips, carrots, oats and fruits. Parts of me kept saying 'something is missing!' However, I knew that it was working something greater than my original food consumptions. I would encourage you to dedicate 21 days of abstaining from heavy foods and focus on the following as an alternative:

- Fruits and vegetables
- Whole grains
- Pseudograins

- Legumes
- Nuts and seeds
- Oats
- Water only

Depending on how many fruits, vegetables, and non-oily/greasy foods you consume, it can have a great impact on your skin. It may feel different for some people who have large portions of foods, yet their skin still seems to look good. However, for others, they may eat a portion of chips and a burger, and the next day, breakouts will occur. Let's focus on the foods that are not advisable to consume for the 21 Days Daniel Fast:

- All animal products including dairy, eggs, fish, meat, and poultry
- Sweeteners whether natural or artificial
- Leavened bread including ingredients such as baking powder, baking soda or yeast
- Refined grains including white flour and white rice
- Processed foods including those containing artificial flavours or preservatives
- Refined oils including canola, corn and soybean

- Alcohol, coffees and teas (I was about to have a peppermint tea at one point!)
- Deep fried foods such as McDonalds, Burger King, local chicken/fish and chips shops

Source: allrecipes.com

It is important to know the type of skin you have which will be covered in chapter 4. I would not recommend rushing to get several products simply because other people are using it. Take a few minutes to ponder on the following steps:

- *Step 1* – have you done enough research before you rush into the checkout online?
- *Step 2* – have you identified what type of ingredients are suitable for your skin type?
- *Step 3* – are you drinking more water and thinking positively?

All these steps contribute to the results of flawless skin; however, you must remember that no matter what the status of your skin is, you are still beautiful beyond what you assume. Do not allow breakouts or skin insecurities to deter you from being who you've been called to be.

Confident Face

There are many people who are waiting on you. What you are going through with your skin is someone else's testimony of when they once had breakouts. At times, when we come to a place in our lives where our skin is flawless and the spots and blemishes are gone, pride gradually starts to take over. Do not get me wrong; it is important to celebrate, but remember when you started in a low state and someone helped you gain confidence with your skincare. Why not use what you've learnt and pass it on to the next person?

There will be times where you feel out of place with new products when using them for a couple of days. This is normal; nonetheless, be intentional about sticking to your preferred routine and not changing products in haste. At times, we lack the patience because our minds are desperate for quick results because it can be a massive struggle for those who are in the season of skin transition.

The eagerness to see change in our skin will take a lot of patience, persistence and perseverance, however, *the beauty is in the waiting*. I've learnt to embrace the journey of waiting, and can confidently say that it's positively impacted the way I view life and contributes to my well-being. If we don't take our time to nurture patience, we will be like the man who looks at himself in the mirror and when he goes back to see himself, he forgets how he looks; reference scripture: James 1:24.

Confident Face

It is important that you control the unreliable emotions within that want to control every aspect of your life. You can't always allow your feelings to win. Put them in their place and take control over your mind. The scripture that has been encouraging me is Romans 8:6 (NIV) which says "The mind governed by the flesh is death, but the mind governed by the Spirit is *life* and *peace.*"

You have to be intentional about feeding your Spirit over your feelings, especially when it comes to the way you take words in. I know how important your skin is to you, however, you must speak life into what you desire to see, rather than feed it with insecurities.

***

IMPORTANT: I don't believe in promoting a life that is easy where everything we desire is going to fall right in front of us.

***

If you had the best skin and didn't go through the anxious tensions of being your own problem-solver, would you really know how to appreciate where you are right now? So many people assume that having life go the way they expect will make them happy, not realising that an easy life leads to a complacent life.

Confident Face

Of course, no one wants to struggle, have bad days, have multiple spots or be mentally and emotionally unhealthy, however, if these areas in our lives did not exist, how would we be able to grow in wisdom and help those coming after us cope? We must learn by nurturing and taking care of our minds constantly; being focused on ONE day at a time.

It is frustrating trying to hold everything together, while you can desperately feel yourself breaking down. Not only that, allowing the restless anxiety to cause further breakouts is an added issue that must be avoided at all costs. Our skin needs time to heal and nurture itself. This includes:

o *A higher level of thinking* – this is a **compulsory** factor. A high mindset leads to greater results.
o *Investing in personal development* – you need time for you; those 20 goals you wanted to reach in a day can be spread out within 14 days. Give yourself a break!
o *Taking regular breaks off social media* – not every online post is real; be sure to apply wisdom.
o *Taking rest when your body tells you to* – and not feeling guilty about it; your body does need rest; it's part of the healing process, so make sure you take short naps wherever needed.

o ***Eating and drinking healthily*** – our food and consumption activities contribute to our level of productivity. Eat well and drink well (in moderation.)

My skin has been through its challenges; however, I am determined to ensure that I constantly do my research, monitor my eating habits and ensure I am constantly drinking water. Our skin protects us against illness and bacteria, which is why it's important to look after it. I am sure you have friends or know people that have dealt with skincare issues for years. If you are reading this book and have not experienced drastic skincare problems, thank God for your life.

It takes a lot of strength when someone is confident and bold enough to stand in front of the mirror and say "I know who I am, regardless of my skin condition!" It takes strength to persevere, despite what societies standards are, tempting you to fit in their own criteria of 'skin success' or 'skin goals.'

The only goal and success you need starts from within. If one is not careful, they will allow society to chase them up the wall and become what they are not. As you continue living your life, there will come a day and time where you refuse to be moved by what other people say or tell you to do.

Confident Face

It is not that you are arrogant, but you must be wise and discerning enough to know what is feeding you and what isn't feeding you, being able to disregard it and know when to speak.

***

IMPORTANT: Do not wait for anyone to believe in you. Show up and let others be influenced by you!

***

Let this sink in because it applies to your own skincare routine as well. I was constantly battling back and forth on what products to use because it felt easier to listen to others, rather than taking the time to sit still and patiently listen to the inner voice, tune my mind and heart to what is right, rather than what *feels* right. *What you know* and *how you feel* are always in battle. One always wants to override the other because it feels easier to tell others what to do rather than take responsibility for yourself. This is an area that we all fall short of, whether we want to admit it or not.

When it comes to our skin, we have to nurture it with tender loving care, so that it will continue to remain healthy. The environments you get yourself into may not always be conducive towards your skin's progress. It may take some time, but you will get there; be patient with your skin and your skin will be patient with you. Don't try to over exfoliate and assume that it's the solution to perfect skin. No matter what comes your way, the new products that appear on the market must be taken into thoughtful consideration before investing.

To add onto this, *take responsibility for your own influence*. It may take months, years or even decades to understand this, but with time, it will sink in. Do not allow the opinions of others to change the way you perceive yourself. What may be good for one may not be good for the other. Live your life in a way that not only influences others regarding their skincare routines, but helps them to identify what works for them.

We must be accountable for what we say, what we use and how we allow it to impact others. We may never know the deep stories that people go through with their skin journey, but we do understand the importance of being accountable to how we feel, which in turns brings a newness to how our skin looks and ultimately helps us function with ease of mind.

Your skin is a reflection of your thoughts; I never knew how important this was until I understood the countless breakouts my face encountered at the time. We may not realise it now, but our thoughts contribute to our wellbeing, but it also portrays negative outcomes if we keep consuming negativity.

Confident Face

Sometimes you will be asked questions such as "why are you always positive?" or "nothing seems to get to you." They don't know how much it costs to be you because they see your smile and how you carry yourself with grace and ease, but they don't fully know what you are going through.

Our skin contributes to how we treat others, because when we see our skin glowing and looking healthy, it is a sign that our mindsets are being utilised, disciplined and developed in helping those around us. When you have spots on your face that unexpectedly appear, you will realise the impact it has on your self-esteem.

I am aware that not everyone has been through skincare issues, however, for those who understand what it is to constantly keep asking when will this season in my life be over – you are reading the right book! It's easy to hear "don't give up!" and yet, feels difficult to work on your skin, focus on the present and be patient for a great future.

I'll leave you with this; in order for your skin to work in your favour, your thought patterns have to continually adapt a consistent attitude of come what may; I know who I am and in due season, I will see change! SPEAK what you want to see, because it's your words that bring the change.

2

o

Why I broke out drastically

It takes a person with vision and unswerving confidence to make a new concept succeed.

One of the reasons my face broke out drastically was due to the inconsistent changes in my skincare routine. I got to a crossroad where I didn't know what to do with the spots and was informed that product A would work with product B, combining it with product C, but to no avail. At the time I broke out, I didn't have a consistent routine and thought using multiple products would help.

I remember using Mario Badescu! My oh my, was it strong!! It felt very harsh on my skin (which I thought at the time was doing what it was meant to do.) To my surprise, it made my skin break out twice as much, as it initially did with the other products I used. I realised that what may work for one person may not work for the other, and had to take it on board.

At the time when you are vulnerable and want a quick fix, your mind isn't focused on patience. It is more focused on seeing results. I am aware that every skincare brand or company desires to become best-sellers in their respective industries, however, it is critical to do research and find out what type of products suit your own skin. It is easy to listen to people and become complacent and eventually end up spending more for nothing. I had severe breakdowns, to the extent of not going out because I knew people would ask what was wrong with my skin.

There was no way I could hide the flaws or the spots. I wouldn't say my spots were huge, but they covered the majority of my face which had an impact on my mental and emotional confidence.

Another reason as to why I broke out drastically was the pressure of people pleasing. In my first book, *It's Time to Heal*, I briefly spoke about the separation of a friend that I dismissed because of the mental and emotional strain it had in my second year of university, whilst balancing my studies and commuting to London every weekend.

I deliberately made the decision to let go and set myself free from the toxic environment I'd been in at the time, and focus solely on my degree. I had to discipline my thoughts daily, to the extent of being able to let those people who weren't adding value in my life know there will be a healthy boundary between us going forwards. You will get to the point where you understand the beauty in changes including seasonal friendships and environments that don't feed or invest in you positively. When my skin started to break out, that was the opportunity to change my life around and make decisions that suited my well-being, and not at the expense of what others wanted me to do or become. As I looked at myself in the mirror, I had a 1-2-1 and said that I literally had enough. This included wearing no make-up, drinking water consistently, and having up to eight hours of sleep each night. I had to make a conscious decision, because if I didn't, I'd be deceiving myself. This is something I encourage you to partake in.

A good night's rest is critical to great performance, health and mental stability. Do not neglect rest, no matter how preoccupied life is for you; you are important and you need to make sure you are looking after yourself. When you stand in the mirror, what do you see? Does your skin look flawless or are new spots appearing? Have you taken the time to acknowledge the changes in your eating habits that could be causing the unexpected reactions?

Now, hear me when I say this: you may never know the impact and attachment one has on a friend, which affects ones' self-esteem. Allowing someone to have power over you is not only detrimental to the mind, but also to your physical attributes. To add on this, allowing too many people to speak into your life about what you should or shouldn't use is detrimental and should be taken with caution.

Yes, there are people who genuinely want to help by supporting, but if one is not careful, it can seem like manipulation, because there is only so much you can do for someone, and it's their decision to accept it. Do not end up becoming spitefully disrespectful about the other party if they don't agree with your decision. It is not every advice you take from people, because what may work for them may not work for you. Do not be discouraged when it seems as if nothing is happening, or the products you use doesn't seem to work.

Breaking out drastically can also be caused by overanalysing thoughts, and repeating past failures constantly. Yes, because of our human nature, it's easy to go over our wrongs, however it is important to ensure you grant yourself the care needed to avoid carrying more than you can bear. I've experienced seasons where my mind would dwell on failures and how they'd caused me to shrink, rather, I should have used them as a comeback to rise.

Hebrews 10:38 (NIV) says: *"But my righteous one will live by faith, and I take no pleasure in the one who shrinks back."* This spoke very clearly to me due to the fact that God is not pleased when our thoughts keep dwelling on our failures; rather, we should not throw away our confidence because it will be richly rewarded (v35.) Why is it easy to be confident one day and complacent another day? *#stayconsistentalways!*

***

IMPORTANT: If you do not know how to rise from failure, you will attract more failure your way!

***

Remember, the past doesn't need permission to enter your life unless you allow it to; it should be an opportunity to take valuable lessons and learn from it; you must be intentional about what you entertain. In other words, you are responsible for your thoughts. As I mentioned previously, *too many products equal too many chemicals being mixed up*, meaning the layers of your skin can't properly function which becomes inflamed, dry or being consumed with oil.

I hear from time to time that *'less is more'* and I fully agree! I never knew that less was more until I was recommended *Asepso soap* from my dear mother after coming back from Dubai in August 2019. I wanted to change my skincare routine and kept the faith that the Asepso soap would work, despite it being very inexpensive. At the time, I was skeptical on products that were very cheap, but to my surprise, the soap worked very well. The best decision to switch from Garnier gel cleanser was a massive highlight for me. Although I was a consistent user of the Garnier brand, I noticed it started working against my skin. The only product I use from Garnier is the *Pure Active Micellar Water* cleanser.

Within two months, the soap made my spots, blackheads and blemishes fade. I was more confident in leaving the house without make up because of it. I am aware that as you are reading this book, you can look back over your life and see how far you've come with your skincare routine, whether you are currently going through severe breakouts, or have overcome them. No matter what stage you are in, remember that you are not alone.

Breakouts will happen, and whether we want to admit it or not, the majority, if not all of us have been through situations where they've felt uncomfortable to talk about their skincare insecurities. It's easier to feel concerned especially when the first thing people notice is your face as you step outside or have an online meeting (Covid-19 has made it very comfortable alongside Zoom meetings!) However, do you know what else people see?

- Your character
- Your attitude
- Your personality

Confident Face

Let's not forget. We should not always feel the need to focus on the external but how we respond to circumstances beyond our control. You may have a pretty face, but an unattractive attitude will not keep you standing. It doesn't matter what you are going through; you need to remember you are beautiful regardless.

Do not limit yourself because of how you feel. For a temporary moment, what you are going through can be dealt with effectively, but *you must give it time*. Think of it this way and answer the following questions:

What facial cleanser are you currently using?

_____

What toner are you currently using?

_____

What moisturising cream are you currently using?

_____

What serum are you currently using?

_____

What SPF cream are you currently using?

_____

Confident Face

How long have you been using your facial products for?
Circle the appropriate answer:

1 – 2 months   3 – 5 months   6 months +

If you circled *1 – 2 months*, you must understand that it requires patience to see a difference, depending on the type of skin you have. I remember having a number of blackheads that took up to three months, to be precise, to get rid of. When you initially start using a new product, it may irritate your skin at first, because your skin may not be used to the abrupt change.

Unless indicated otherwise, some products depending on the ingredients, can be effective which enables change to start its work. Regardless of how long it takes, be kind to your skin and to yourself. It may work in a month or two for another person, but that does not mean that it won't work for you in the long run. It is a process that takes time and there is beauty in waiting.

If you circled *3 – 5 months*, this is the ideal timeframe for the products to work effectively on your skin without changing or mixing them with other facial products *(it's the consistency that matters!)*

Confident Face

Each product used includes several chemicals that may or may not work for your face. For example, before you use anything with **benzoyl peroxide**, ensure that you speak with your GP or dermatologist about it. I use Duac once daily gel *(which includes 5% of benzoyl peroxide)* prescribed by my GP. I remember when purchasing a one-off product that was similar to Duac from a local chemist, which started reacting on my skin harshly.

I discontinued using it and waited for the re-stocking of the Duac gel. With consistent use of the same products, you are guaranteed to see better results. I was intentional with my facial products and noticed changes within three to five months. I recorded a video on my YouTube channel (*Esther N J*) about my skincare routine. Take the time to watch it and see the way my skin changed between June to October 2019. I am still on a journey and am learning to embrace change and adapt the right mindset to suit my skincare requirements.

If you circled *6 months+*, depending on the severity of your skin, this could be the ideal timeframe it will take if one has *cystic acne, nodular acne*, or *nodulocystic acne*. Regardless of what sort of skin condition you have, be confident and expectant that it will go, despite the delay. Do not allow the fear of how your skin looks *in a season* to make you give up.

Confident Face

Your skin won't always be the way you desire it to be, and I had to learn this during my time at university. Another reason it may take time for our skin to change is due to *family genes.* Perhaps your parents, grandparents or great grandparents had the issue of dealing with intense skincare experiences. This doesn't mean it has to follow you throughout the rest of your days.

Remember, it is just a season, not a lifetime, depending on how well you take care of your skin. I am aware that spots and acne are two different types of conditions, however, I want to focus more on acne, so let's take a deeper look into the definitions of the different types:

1) ***Cystic acne***: this is where the pores in the skin become blocked and leads to inflammation and irritation – *Source: healthline.com.*

2) ***Nodular acne***: a more severe form of acne that causes deep issues within the skin and may persist within weeks and months eventually hardening into cysts – *Source: healthline.com.*

3) ***Nodulocystic acne***: this is where acne affects not only your face, but your back and chest. *Source: dermnetnz.org.*

Confident Face

No matter what type of acne you have, remember that it is possible to get rid of them. It may not go away immediately, but you have to cultivate patience and give your skin time to adapt with the changes. At times, when we touch our faces, that is what causes bacteria, and the environments we are in that creates dirt to trap pores and eventually becoming blocked. In turn, it creates spots turned into acne and transforms to blackheads.

Your insecurities are birthing confidence in God; the One that made you in His image. There is beauty in brokenness, whether it is blemishes on your skin, breakouts on your body or scars that may never go away. You are more than a bruise. You are more than a spot. You are more than acne.

You are more than society's standards of beauty. You are more! You are coming out of your struggles! You are coming out of your situations! You are coming out of your flaws! You are not your hyperpigmentation! You are who God says you are! It may take a while to agree, but you have to keep going and believing it will get better.

I remember going to my friend's house and we had a great conversation which made me bring up these three words: *"own your season!"* These words can be used in different ways i.e. maintaining your single season and enjoying it to the fullest. Finding purpose in singleness is the best place to be.

Confident Face

You must enjoy each step of the way life is going without putting heavy pressure on yourself. The reasons why we tend to break out is because we become *more* loyal to what people say rather than what God knows about us.

When it comes to breaking out on the skin, it is important to identify the root matter. It may not always be the products that causes breakouts. At times, it can be our own thoughts, what we listen to and who has our ear. Has it occurred to you that what you listen to can have an impact both positively or negatively? In other words, you have to control who speaks into your life because not everyone has the right to. Words spoken are powerful and have great meaning.

There comes a time where we must analyse those in our lives by understanding who *feeds us* and who *needs us*. Bishop TD Jakes in one of his sermons on YouTube informed to write a list of people who feed and need us. He mentioned that if the list of feeders is lower than the needers, there must be accountability taken for it.

In other words, those who need you tend to be liabilities, and those who feed you are assets. Let's break it down further:

NEEDERS: Those who **NEED** you + people who take and consume time, energy and information from you =
LIABILITY!

Confident Face

FEEDERS: Those who **FEED** you + people who invest in your well-being, character and brings out the best in you by adding value = **ASSET!**

Could it be at the time I was breaking out drastically, that my mind was consuming many opinions of other people's perspectives? We must learn to discern what is being spoken into our lives and be accountable for how much we consume. This can be one aspect of skin breakouts if too much overload is being placed in our minds. Assets add value, but liabilities steal your joy. Nonetheless, I believe there are many ways that others have broken out on their skin. Write down your experiences about a time on you broke out drastically:

_____

_____

_____

_____

_____

How did you find that? Therapeutic right?! It is very important to ensure that when you heed to someone's advice, you are intentional and selective on what works for you. You are to be responsible for what you listen to and the impact it has on your purchasing patterns. You have to create financial boundaries on how much you spend and utilise, until you are ready to invest in more expensive products. Ask yourself what steps you are willing to take to ensure your thoughts are healthy. It is important to know what to accept and what to reject. Don't be the individual that is easily accustomed to accepting anything, and take the time to know your skin abilities.

We may never realise that our breakouts are signs of change and transformation. When you've been in a certain situation for a length of time, it's time to switch it up. If you are constantly lacking responsibility and not being intentional about your own journey, it is not in your right to put the blame on others. The way you act will determine how others will operate around you. We must understand that the solution is how we respond to our feelings.

3

o

What causes your face to get spots?

Your moment defines you - how you deal with that moment will determine who you are.

Acne is caused by bacteria which tends to stay on the skin if not taken care of appropriately. The follicles in the skin where hair grows become clogged with oil and dead skin cells, and the bacteria eventually starts to spread. If you have a spot on your skin, it may hurt for some time, become swollen and eventually turn quite hot when touching it unnecessarily. Eventually, the walls of the follicles start to break down which affects the skin cells and bacteria, and eventually forms a pimple. (Source: *Mayo Clinic.*)

When I did thorough research on what causes spots to break out on the skin, I was inspired by how it actually started. When washing your face or using a face steamer, you can see how clean your pores are. The moment you move around, it accumulates dust and bacteria that penetrates on the skin without realising it. However, according to Jasmina

Aganovic, she stated that there are good bacteria's that we can take advantage of:

"Your skin is colonized by millions and millions of bacteria, viruses, and fungi, and just like the microbes in your gut have a larger impact on overall health, microbes on your skin, which is your largest organ, impact the way it looks and feels and its ability to serve as a barrier between your body and the outside world."

When I saw this, it made me think. Can we ever be in an environment where everything is 100% clean? *The greatest factor to know is that your skin is always working to your advantage, whether you believe it or not.* Despite spots appearing randomly, remember, they will not be there forever. It will end, just like certain seasons in our lives have to end in order for new doors of opportunity to be presented to us.

***

IMPORTANT: If you keep saying your spots will never go away, the truth is, they won't. Your words are extremely powerful, and what you speak, carries weight!

***

Confident Face

In addition to this, I remember my sister encouraging me not to pick my spots each time I saw one pop up, however, it wasn't easy to do. I knew that picking one spot would lead to another, but due to the irritation, I wanted them all gone. One of the reasons I am sharing this is because at times, we can be very impatient, wanting everything to go our way and having expectations on how we should look. Picking spots, let alone touching your face is what attracts dirt and bacteria. Ultimately, this leads to spots and eventually leaves scarring from the picking.

As we deal with severe spot breakouts from time to time, I know the frustration and how they come and go. One day, you see a small spot gradually becoming larger, but I guarantee that when you don't focus on it, the spot gradually become smaller as you aren't giving your emotions power to think in an unhealthy way. This is one of the reasons why we must renew our minds because healing and restoration starts within.

In essence, sleeping with make-up causes severe breakouts! I remember at university doing this and the next day when I woke up, my skin broke out. When our pores become inflamed and clogged, particularly around the T-Zone (*forehead, nose and chin*), this is when spots gradually start to appear. Let's take another look at other contributing factors that cause spots:

Confident Face

Hair products

Pay attention to the hair products you use. It is important that we keep our hair healthy by being aware of certain products that contain harsh chemicals not suitable for the scalp. Currently, I am using an effective hair oil called Inches from Planted (www.thisisplanted.com) which promotes hair growth. If you use any type of hair oil before going to bed, give it time to sink in to the scalp before resting on the pillow to prevent it from spreading, causing spots. I also use Shea Moisture's Munuka Honey and Mafura oil shampoo and conditioner range, and it's been good so far.

Make-up brushes

I never used to think this was the case, but as my skin constantly looks for ways to improve, I understand the importance of washing my make-up brushes each time I use them. Depending on how often you wear make-up, your brushes also contain bacteria. As mentioned above, if you wear make-up to bed, you are more likely to get spots on your skin. Washing your make-up brushes may be a long process, but it is enjoyable if you take the time to do it consistently, and in turn, reduce the amount of make-up. Getting your eyebrows shaped and applying a nice clear lipgloss will suffice.

Confident Face

Too many facial cleansers

I must admit, this was me in university! I used various cleansers that eventually didn't help at all. I was not focused on the ingredients used; I was moved by what others thought of the products and decided to take it from there. If you don't take the time to research for applicable and specific products suitable for your skin type, you are more likely to break out.

When you know your skin type, it is a great advantage, particularly for those who react quite harshly. Cleansers with strong fragrances may disagree with your skin type. There are several ways to avoid drastic breakouts by speaking to a dermatologist or visiting your local GP and see what recommendations can be given.

Your phone

When Covid-19 started in the UK, I didn't realise the impact that mobile phones had towards our skin. With that being said, I was consistently using antibacterial wipes to clean my phone. This is important because different products contaminate our phones, making it spread towards the skin and cause bacteria. It is important to clean your phone, especially the headphones and airpods. This will help avoid breakouts especially on the cheeks.

Confident Face

Stress and overthinking

The more you desire to control every area of your life, the more you attract restless thoughts and fears that are not necessary. This has become one of the biggest contributing factors as to why stress and endless thoughts occur. I remember a time where my thoughts were inconsistent, trying to resolve issues that had not even occurred yet. It made me realise that the more I was dwelling on those thoughts, the more I started seeing various breakouts on my face. Investing in skincare is important, as well as investing in your physical and mental health. The solution is to *be still and relax*, whilst feeding your mind with positive thoughts. Words of elevation, wisdom and growth are daily nutrients.

Family genes

Depending on family genes, it can also have an impact on ones' skin. If you, or a family member have experienced breakouts in the past, it is more likely that it can happen to another immediate member. This is normal and should not be overlooked, and will eventually go with time. It is important, however, to do your research with regards to why spots occur, especially when you least expect them to appear.

Confident Face

No matter what you are going through, it is only for a season. Do not make permanent decisions based on temporary situations. You could wake up one day and have a big spot; in the next few weeks, it will eventually get smaller. In other words, do not feed your weaknesses but overpower them by being consistent in your skincare routine.

Having a consistent skincare routine is vital, especially times where the skin changes due to the environment and weather conditions. I mentioned that our mental and eating habits play a dramatic role in the process of how our skin operates in chapter 1. Do not take your skin for granted, especially if you haven't experienced acne or breakouts.

Another contributing factor that affects your skin is the power of your words. Proverbs 18:21 reminds us that *"the power of life and death is in the tongue."* If you do not know how to speak positively in your life, how will you be able to embrace and fight the bigger issues of life?

To add on this, it is important to take the time to invest in yourself, withdrawing from the crowds and find your safe place (I call it *the Secret Place.*) Speak to your Maker about your troubles and anxious thoughts. The more consistent you are in doing this with Him, the better you will become in your mindset and throughout your skincare routines.

Confident Face

IMPORTANT: You need time for you!

***

No one is going to fight your battles like you will. No matter what countless thoughts are entering your mind, you must learn to discipline the lies, the fears and the anxieties of "I can't" to "I CAN!" It is very possible! We use the concept of *I CAN* to remind people of their value and worth. At times, it can be overlooked due to what our minds are consumed with. The same way no one is going to cure your spots unless you take the practical steps.

Refuse to feel sorry for yourself; that is how you remain complacent and entertain self-pity. We must avoid the temptation to be defined by our current status and learn to make peace with the process. Endeavour to embrace your season and learn from it as it will help you grow each day.

***

IMPORTANT: Do not rush any good thing, unless you want it to be a bad thing!

***

Throughout 2020, I learnt about the beauty of patience in several areas of my life; my skincare routine, business, family and friends, and more importantly, working on becoming better. 2020 has taught us a lot of hard lessons. One of them is to work effectively in uncertainty and use what we have to make an impact. When you carry toxic thoughts around, it prevents you from seeing results because of fear. Don't allow anything to get in the way of your progress because it is preparing you for the breakthrough moment.

There is a time and season for everything, and that includes dealing with several insecurities, including the ones that are hidden from others. Remember, we all have days where our skin won't co-operate. In my book *The Power of a Forward-Thinking Mindset*, I place emphasis on *faith* and taking practical steps to help the reader move forwards with their life by not dwelling on the past, but seeing it as a catalyst to push them into destiny. This is the same approach we should have in being confident with our own skin and loving who God made us to be.

At times, if we are not careful, we can be our own obstacles, because our thoughts and unravelling, restless minds tend to block our way, making it difficult to not only function within, but eventually affect those we care about. This in turns gives a negative outlook and doesn't bring about the confidence needed. When it comes to the way we consume words and our actions show through, we must ensure that it doesn't have an impact on our physical health.

Spots may not always go away when we want them to, but it does teach us how to look after ourselves. Anytime you are feeling overwhelmed and tempted to pick your spots, ask yourself in a few days' time whether you'll be happy with the outcome. Be intentional with your skin and take the time to nurture and look after it. Get into a healthy habit of sleeping on time, eating well and cultivating good thoughts that will give your skin a healthy look now and for the future.

Countless scrolling on social media is one of the most detrimental factors causing millennials to question who they are, making them feel insecure and being a counterfeit version of who they've been called to be. To the world, you should be a certain look, type, height, width, structure, etc. To God, He wants you to come as you are; to strip off the weight. When deception comes and paints itself to be confident, without discernment, it's easy to be swayed by what we see and hear. When it becomes all too much, this is where spots start appearing.

When you listen to others and allow them to have influence over you, it is difficult to make your own decision. Learn to take rest. Balance your life with God's truth and not social demands. Society isn't working on your personal development. Discipline and balance are vital.

4

○

What is your skin type?

The difference in you is the difference you make in the world.

No matter the type of skin you have, it is your responsibility to know what works best for you and what doesn't. Nonetheless, I've noticed that my skin works extremely well in the winter periods. Due to the harshness of cold weather seasons, I must ensure that my skin is frequently moisturised without over applying several products. When it comes to your skin type, I want you to consider and answer the following questions:

- Does changing facial products frequently make you react within a week i.e. 7 days? Explain your reason:

_____

_____

Confident Face

- Do you feel a sting when using products including the ingredient *benzoyl peroxide?*

_____

_____

- How many products are you using each day and night? (overuse of products can cause severe breakouts)

_____

_____

- Can you stick to one routine at a time and see how it works from there?

_____

_____

- Do you touch your face at unnecessary times?

How did the above go? What did you learn from writing your answers, and how will you apply them going forwards? The mistake we make at times, is looking at someone else's skin and assuming what they use will work for us.

If you have *combination skin*, it is important to ensure that products containing natural ingredients help to produce a healthy balance. Your skin will change, and as you grow older, your body starts to adapt. There are also internal and external factors to consider when identifying your skin type. When you consume foods that contain high levels of oil and refined/sugary ingredients, it can have an impact on your skin.

What you feed your body with will eventually be shown outwardly. I remember when I took a break from eating meat for a month, and although my body didn't feel the same, I gradually saw positive changes in my skin. This is the same with cutting down on carbs, sweets and chocolates. My body knows when I've changed my diet regime and how it adapts. I am also open to plant-based foods once in a while, notwithstanding, I still enjoy different types of meats. When it comes to your skin feeling out of place, do not ignore it. When washing your face, depending on your skin type, the product eventually removes dead skin. This is a good sign. When the skin comes off, it helps to create a new surface of skin. According to the *American Academy of Dermatology Association* (AADA) they state that there are *three layers* of skin types which are:

1) **Epidermis** – which is the top layer of the skin that is **seen**
2) **Dermis** – which is the thicker layer of skin that benefits your body
3) **Subcutaneous fat** – which is the bottom layer of the skin that is **unseen**

All these layers of skin types are important, however, what is vitally crucial is how you treat skin that is unseen. The *subcutaneous fat* is what keeps the skin from becoming too cold or too hot. In other words, it balances your skin to ensure that it is functioning effectively. I had severe frost bite in primary school which made my fingers extremely numb.

I was thankful for my classroom that had large radiators and could put my little fingers on it to ease the pain. I washed my hands with lukewarm water. Eventually, I felt my fingers again, whilst the subcutaneous fat helped my fingers become warm, and was good that I took the relevant action on time.

Confident Face

With regards to the different types of skin we have, nonetheless, subcutaneous fat varies. Some individuals have thick skin, whilst others have tender, more sensitive skin. This is where *dermis* comes in, because it can create sweat depending on how the body functions.

Have you noticed that when some individuals walk, they sweat quicker than others? This is because the dermis is described as little pockets called *sweat glands* that go through little tubes and come out of holes known as 'pores' according to the *American Academy of Dermatology Association* (AADA.) When you wash your face with warm water, the pores begin to gradually open.

For *epidermis*, it is the thinnest (sensitive) part of the skin. This includes our eyelids, for example. We know how much care to take when it comes to washing our eye area. This type of skin is exposed to the sun which gives colour and produces melanin. It also protects your immune system and keeps the body healthy. In effect, what isn't seen must be worked on twice as much as what is seen.

We all have different skin types, and it is important to identify what works well with your skin and what doesn't. I enjoy using what I already know works well for my skin. Due to our skin changing each time, we must take accountability for the results it brings. Our skin plays a pivotal role in building inner confidence. Let's take a look at the following:

- ***Keeping a healthy balanced diet*** – what you eat has a massive impact on your skin. It can produce acne, blemishes and dark spots. Make sure you are having fruit and vegetables and cutting down on oily produces.

- ***Keep drinking water*** – (I will expand on this in chapter 8). When you don't drink water regularly, the skin eventually loses its moisture. Drinking water helps to boost your immune system whilst helping your skin remain supple and fresh.

- ***Moisturise moisturise moisturise*** – when the weather is hot; moisturise. When the weather is cold; moisturise. You need to find the right moisturising cream or serum that is suitable for your skin type.

- ***Be kind to yourself*** – this is a very crucial part in the journey of good skincare. Short, yet powerful. Be kind to yourself; be kind to your skin, for it will surely pay off.

Confident Face

Change is inevitable. You can have oily skin in your 20s and dry skin in your 30s. Nonetheless, you must be intentional in looking after it. I remember speaking to a friend and we were discussing about the property market, how inflation and tax are constantly increasing.

In the same way these factors are increasing, our minds should be positioned to think higher. When situations around you seem difficult to understand, re-position your mindset. It's not enough to allow the situations to defeat and cause you to remain stagnant. No one knows your thoughts the way you do.

Your skin changes in accordance with your thoughts, and you must be intentional about monitoring its progress. Your skin type may change, but it doesn't mean your attitude or character should. When you build a positive community around you, others will be attracted to it and adapt with you. The only way is forwards, so make sure you are heading that way with your skincare routine and more importantly, your thoughts.

5

o

What you need to know about your skin

Change is inevitable – and so is your skin.

Life changes, therefore, our skin changes. You can have great skin in one season; another season, it may not work in your favour. No matter how it seems, our skin is constantly being impacted by our environment and the thoughts we consume. Regardless, it is your responsibility to look after your skin. I've made it easy for you to differentiate between dry skin, normal/combination skin and oily skin:

DRY SKIN

According to tatcha.com, it states that dry skin is largely due to genetics and environmental factors including our lifestyle and diets, hormonal changes and the current climate. Are you aware that not drinking enough water has an impact on your skin feeling dry? It is important to have at least 2 litres of water a day to keep you and the body hydrated. Water helps to keep moisture in the skin.

Confident Face

Depending on the cleanser you use, it is important to make sure the ingredients are *non-abrasive* to help promote skin cell turnover without removing the skin's natural oils as this is what makes the skin dry.

NORMAL/COMBINATION SKIN

If you fall into this category, using the right moisturisers will keep the skin healthy. Gel-based moisturises are good for skin absorption and less likely to cause several breakouts. If you have normal to combination skin, the good fact about using an oil or serum that includes Vitamin C is that it brightens the skin whilst fighting acne and bacteria to prevent new spots from forming.

When using an oil or serum, it's best to start with a small amount, depending on how the skin feels at the time prior to applying. For example, when washing my face, I have to use a toner before applying my Vitamin C oil or serum to keep my skin moisturised.

OILY SKIN

Oily skin can take a long time to overcome due to food consumption, family genes and other environmental factors. Excessive oily skin can leave pores unclogged and congested that it doesn't help the skin to breathe.

There are times where your skin may be oily throughout the day. In order to prevent this from happening, it is recommended to use a *blotting paper* (which can be purchased in any drugstore) and use it on your forehead, cheeks and chin.

Once this is done, use natural light to observe how much oil is on the blotting paper. If the oil covers the majority of the blotting paper, you are more likely to have excessive oily skin. Having oily skin is also prone to *Post-Inflammatory Hyperpigmentation,* also known as (PIH) which is a condition that leaves dark spots on the skin after a breakout.

Being consistent with your exfoliation routine will help lighten dark spots by working on the uppermost layers of the skin and reveal new cells. Depending on how oily or intense your skin is, don't use multiple products at once as your skin naturally produces its own oil.

***

REMEMBER: You do not want to cover up oil with oil.

***

In as much as society portrays a lot of focus on how we should look, every part of our body is important as well. 1 Corinthians 12:21 says that: *"The eye cannot say to the hand 'I don't need you!' and the head cannot say to the feet, 'I don't need you!'"* No matter what decisions are made, our bodies need every part of it to work effectively. When we are tempted to neglect other parts of our skin, it becomes a gradual insecurity that develops overtime. On the other hand, we are conscious that when we encounter people, their first focus is our face or how we look (which is true!) I would be surprised if someone walking in front me decides to watch my feet first. Oh my, that would be awkward!

Although this is true, we must learn to nurture every part of our body, from our knees to our knuckles and every part of our being. When you encounter spots and blackheads on your chest or back, it's a good opportunity to research on certain products including body washes, fragrance-free soaps and utilising home-made natural remedies.

According to the **www.mydcsi.com** blog (Feb 2020), it includes the benefits of salt water. If you have oily skin, you can benefit from washing your face and body with mild salt water because it includes moisture-reducing abilities to control excess oil and clogged pores. If you have sensitive skin, however, salt water should be used for the body, keeping it clean and protected.

Your skin needs a healthy balance of moisture, and it is important to know the different types of products to use. Salt water restores the skin's natural pH balance and removes impurities that promote new skin growth.

Confident Face

Whilst it is vital to look after your internal organs, it will eventually show up on your skin, especially when not taking responsibility on the number of food consumptions, sugars and oil used – *Source: newsinhealth.nih.gov.*

Takeaways are increasingly popular; however, it is better to know what ingredients are being used, therefore, utilising the opportunity to cook from home is a huge benefit for skincare goals and financial wisdom. What may work for one person may not work for the other, and your skin can easily adapt to what you're used to. Once you find a remedy, stick to the routine.

Let's talk about what *you* need to know about your skin:

1) Your skin is working to protect it against all forms of bacteria
2) Your skin needs time to implement new products so be patient and take care of it
3) It is important to get enough sleep for your skin to work in your favour
4) If you become anxious or stressed out easily, it can affect the health of your skin
5) Avoid strong soaps and facial gel cleansers in order to keep the skin supple and soft and avoid it being dry

6) LOVE YOUR OWN SKIN: TAKE GOOD CARE OF IT!

I didn't understand the importance of good skin until I noticed the intense breakouts unexpectedly, to the extent where putting on make-up couldn't help. If you are currently struggling with breakouts, you would know that when applying foundation, seeing those spots and blackheads can cause you to feel uneasy. According to the Eucerin website (www.eucerin.co.uk), it highlights five components that our skin protects us from including:

- **Changes in temperature and humidity**: our skin helps to regulate body temperature whilst controlling moisture loss and maintaining the balance of fluids.

- **Disease**: our skin works to neutralise aggressors such as bacteria, viruses and pollution and prevents them for entering the body.

- **UV rays**: when the skin is over-exposed, it can cause harmful rays which is aggressive molecules that cause cell damage. This is why it is important to apply the right SPF creams and sunscreen.

- **Pressure, blows and abrasion**: our skin recognises pain and alerts us to danger which acts as a barrier and shock absorber.

- **Chemical substances**: our skin is the first line of defence against aggressive formulas we may encounter, either in the workplace, at home, or when outside if we use harsh cleansing products or inappropriate skincare products.

Within the layers of our skin, we may not feel like anything is happening, but it is doing more than we expect. Just like God Himself; we don't see Him physically, but we are assured with faith, confidence and belief, that He is up to something great. I don't know what sort of life you've lived in the past, presently, or the battles you're facing, nonetheless, you are a CONFIDENT FACE!

The greatest opportunities and breakthroughs come when you least expect it. Above all, remind yourself each day that you are more than your flaws. The world can't define who you are, unless you allow it to. I have come too far to look back and allow my skin issues to define me. A song that I enjoy singing from time to time is: "God is working, He's still working; God is working even now – though we often don't know just how; God is working, He's still working; God is working even now!"

It doesn't matter how long it takes; God is working and so is your skin. It's your submission that He is looking for. We must cultivate an attitude of patience in every stage of our lives. You can't be defined by the way you feel at this moment in time because it is a *season*. Whatever is happening in our lives, we know at some point, it will come to an end.

Another key factor you must know about your skin is that it works better when you are in calm and peaceful situations. Do not rush the process when your skin is healing. It's what you learn during the process of healing that matters most.

Your skin will be as beautiful as it is when you start making it a priority. The importance of working on your skin starts with a *fixed mindset*. What practical steps are you going to take to work on your skincare routine? There are several ways you can work on your skin which include the following:

- ***Conduct your own research specifically catered to the nature of your skin*** – facial cleansers for oily skin or dry skin etc.

- ***Be consistent in having regular and appropriate sleeping patterns*** – avoid sleeping late and waking up late – this prevents productivity throughout the day.

- ***Look within yourself*** – what thoughts and words are you speaking into your life? How is this impacting the rest of your face and skin? Remember, it's not about how others see you, but how you see YOU!

- ***Stop overthinking*** – countless thoughts cause serious headaches. Stop giving your feelings power over you!

Be intentional with what goes in your mind as it produces the outcomes of life. When using a different product, you eventually see changes in the first few days, but whilst using it for a couple of weeks, it tends to change the way the skin feels, and in turn, can affect other areas. This has been a major experience for those in particular who have oily and sensitive skin.

When this happens, discontinue using the product. Don't put pressure on yourself because of the amount spent. Your life is far more valuable than any product, and once you remember that, you'll start to appreciate and embrace who you are. When unexpected news occurs, it will trigger the way you see life. This, in turn has an impact on your psychical appearance and will influence the way you treat your body.

In order to overcome the pressure, it will take discipline to work on your thoughts. It always inspires me when those we look up to come out of their comfort zones and share personal experiences of how their skincare journey impacted them, whether positively or negatively. It takes great confidence and strength to do so, and as we continue our individual paths of life, there will be unexpected circumstances, however, you must keep going.

When your skin starts to react unexpectedly, know that it will have to get worse to get better. For those who understand the real anxieties of having breakouts, you'll agree with me. As I was hoping that my skin got better, it started becoming intense, however, that is what pushed me in coming out of my comfort zone, doing my research and learning more about my skin than ever before.

Covid-19 has taught us that life will come with unexpected surprises, but we must keep going regardless of it. You should know by now that you are valuable and shouldn't spread yourself too thin. Work on your mindset, and let your skin continue to do what it needs to do. Being in control over everything is what causes a lot of unnecessary pressure.

Confident Face

You must refuse to worry, because in life, there will always be distractions enticing you to act in a certain way. The temptation to question your own beauty isn't healthy. You have to see your skincare problems as opportunities to become whole within yourself. Don't wait to get advice from people before you make a decision to invest in who you've been called to be.

Remember to add *patience* in your skincare routine; give it time to nurture and grow, and eventually, you will see the results. It's not about rushing the process. Remember your skin can either be dry, normal/combination or oily, however, it is your responsibility to identify what your skin type is and use products suitable for it. Take the time to embrace your skin and allow it to do what it needs to do.

6

o

Is there a one-way solution?

Just because you don't feel anything is happening, doesn't mean nothing is happening!

When it comes to skincare, I don't believe there is a one-way solution to achieving great skin. If there was, by now, everyone we meet would have flawless skin. However, I do believe that finding out what products and ingredients work for each individual is the suitable solution. It's important to understand that what was recommended by a friend or advisor doesn't necessarily mean it will work for you.

I remember the countless adverts and promotions that was used to persuade buyers to purchase Cetaphil Gentle Skin Cleanser and their positive reviews, so I decided to purchase it. I gave it a few weeks to see a difference and ended up with having more breakouts. What did this teach me? To not base my purchasing patterns on what others have described. It's a lesson learnt and something that shouldn't be taken lightly.

Depending on how well one looks after their skin, as long as they have found the right routine that is simple and easy to use, it should be applied consistently. Now, look in the mirror and analyse your face. Focus on what areas you need to work on, starting from your forehead, to your cheeks, to your chin and your neck. I mentioned that your chest is a reflection of how your skin will look if action isn't taken care of properly. I remember having a few spots on my chest and noticed that new spots were appearing on my face.

As mentioned in chapter 5, our skin is always changing, therefore, it's important to have a routine that works for you. Notwithstanding, I am aware that every individual deals with issues and the changes of several products differently. When you take the time to know what skin type you have, and more importantly, involve God in every insecurity about your skin, that is where change truly begins. Just because your spots are visible, doesn't define your beauty. You still ought to love the way you are because it is part of the healing process.

There are other alternatives that people have when it comes to expressing their emotions. Some prefer to write their thoughts on paper. Others prefer participating in spoken word, and many other forms of self-expression. No matter what category you're in, it's imperative that you find what is best for you and ensure it suits your needs. I've asked two ladies to contribute in sharing their personal experiences of what they encountered during their face breakout and the solutions they made to become mentally, emotionally and physically healthy. I won't spoil it and tell you what chapter it's in, so keep on reading…

In life, many attacks, left, right and centre will come your way. Breakouts from the time of the month for women, a hard breakdown from the loss of a loved one, inconsistent eating habits due to stress and anxiety; all these lead to dysfunction. From experience, I know how stress, in particular, had an impact on my skincare routine.

Running around trying to buy the expensive products to help clear my blackheads at the time, and the solution wasn't what I expected. I had to do more than the usual visits to drugstores and depend solely on online research and reviews. I had to seek the One that created me in His image, reminding me that I am who He says I am.

Frustrated seasons will come; you wake up and see a new spot appearing without your consent. It becomes overwhelming which makes it demanding when you are doing it by yourself. However, Matthew 11:28 (NIV) says: *"Come to me, all you who are weary and burdened, and I will give you rest."*

When did you come to the Father with your needs? I am guilty of trying to micro-manage everything in my life, and didn't notice that I eventually became my own god! I assumed in my heart that I could handle it and my solution was the best way.

Confident Face

Note: don't try to figure out everything on your own. You get to a stage in your life where you realise that your way isn't working and decide to surrender it to God. All along, that is what I should've done. The same is for you also. When the burden of trying to find several options to obtain clear skin becomes a burden, STOP! Take time out of your schedule and acknowledge that God is actively present in every area of your life.

Your confidence isn't built when your skin is flawless; your confidence starts when you know that your spots, acne or blackheads doesn't have power over you. You are able to smile again because you know that your best days are ahead of you. It's easy to hear this constantly, but there comes a time when you have to open your mouth and speak into your own life.

We are given each day to live and express how great God is, not to grumble and complain about what isn't working out well. Although it's important to be honest about where you are in life, do not stay there. You are more than you think.

When it comes to finding solutions, it will take many turns, detours and unexpected disruptions if done without wise counsel. When you are in vulnerable situations, you must also learn how to discern those who speak into your life, because when words are spoken, it can't be taken back.

Confident Face

At this moment in time, what thoughts are you harbouring that causes you to doubt and fear? When you constantly believe the lies that come from the past, you end up affecting your future. You ought to shut every door of the past behind and not allow it to change who you are.

The moment the past is opened, if you aren't mentally strong enough, it will rob you of peace, joy and contentment. The saying of: *'don't put your eggs in one basket'* is stated for a reason. If you think one way, you will reap only that one way. Learn to be flexible and adaptable.

I know it's easy to succumb to a certain way of thinking, especially when life is fast-paced, however, we must come to a point in our lives and remind ourselves of who we are in Christ. *There is so much more to you than outer beauty.* There shouldn't be a time in our lives where we feel out of place because of what seems trending.

Trends will come and go, but you will always be your authentic self. It is important that we remember not to feel triggered by a post on social media or feeling pressured in our own minds. The time we have is NOW to think better about who we are, the impact and influence that's embedded in us, and the opportunity to remind others of who they are, lest they forget.

Confident Face

Matthew 18:7 (NIV) says: *"Woe to the world because of the things that cause people to stumble."* There shouldn't be a one-way system that society offers which causes God's children to stumble. Instead, we ought to shine our light and make the difference in our communities.

When vulnerability meets light, it's not comfortable. It prefers to stay in darkness because being comfortable is better than facing your own weaknesses. This shouldn't be the case. Now is the time to *own your flaws*, facing it in confidence, rather than avoiding it.

How we treat others has consequences; causing a brother or sister to doubt who they are, speaking negative words or cultivating toxic thoughts doesn't help. You must understand your own unique responsibility to make positive changes where you can.

If you need to let go of ill-thoughts, you need to find someone you can trust, rather than heaping the burdens on another person. It's some of the reasons why skin breakouts occur because we have not built a confident level of trust within ourselves and placed healthy boundaries on how far one can go in a friendship or relationship.

In the book of John 7:24 (ESV) it says: *"Do not judge by appearances, but judge with the right judgment."* This lets us know that we ought not to judge according to how people look, but to judge with the right lens in love and correction.

Confident Face

The society may convince you to use their methods, but who are you going to listen to? Remember that your skin journey is unique to you, and I will add this as a bonus: *whoever has your ear, has your mind.* Know how much words you are listening to.

We shouldn't get comfortable where we are because there is a lot in us to give. There is pressure to find the right product, the right eye corrector, the right concealer, but no matter what, there will always be a new product or service on the market. The same way companies, brands and organisations strategise to bring new stock and innovate; it would be a good opportunity to look within yourself and be transformed by the renewing of your mind. Your mindset is a powerful asset that can take you further when used wisely.

There is so much you can do to keep striving, searching and worrying yourself about what others are using. I remember a time where an online store was advertising a thick shimmery gold face mask. It was sponsored on Instagram and a lot of comments, reviews and feedback were given on it.

When I clicked on the website, I read the ingredients and asked myself before I decided to make the purchase, 'do I know what I'm putting on my face?' Was it an instant gratification moment to let others know I purchased a facial mask that promised would clear dark spots within a week, for me to be disappointed in the end?

I was happy when I made the decision not to proceed with it, and was content with the products I'd used at the time. Do not allow the pressures of social media or what others are using to deter you from what you already use. What you have is greater and that starts within. Do not underestimate how much you have in **you**. Speak and declare what you believe into your skin, even when it seems to be getting worse.

Every time you allow emotions to get in the way of your skin, it eventually ends up looking bigger than it initially was – a spot that started out small can look bigger due to your perception. Our perceptions matter each time we speak, think and act.

Your words and thoughts practically do their part in helping to avoid the so called 'one-way system' and ultimately, realise that there are different ways to obtain clearer skin. There is freedom in doing what you've been called to do, and not feeling pressure from others.

You may want the easy way out because it's comfortable. However, you must understand that life won't always be one-sided. Life will have seasons where you'll have to adapt to different changes. Thinking one way causes stagnation because a one-sided individual is prone to focus on one side of the story. A wise person is able to identify and learn from two parties and make a concrete decision and not be seen as a biased individual.

A time is coming where decisions must be made to suit your needs. There has to be sound discipline when your plans aren't going the way you expected them to. If you are easily misled by others, it will be difficult to make healthy decisions. Communicate with others in wisdom, and remember to work on your own skincare routine exploring new products that suit you.

7

o

Look Within

Be still and look within.

When you look within yourself, take the time to focus on the following numbers:

Number 1: What thoughts are coming into your mind that causes you to worry?

Number 2: How do you handle situations that unexpectedly appear?

Number 3: Are you appreciating what you have around you?

Number 4: Is it becoming a burden that you can't seem to be thankful for small blessings?

All these thoughts have to be considered as you look within yourself. At times, looking within can be uncomfortable because you are faced with yourself, but it is one of the best ways to overcome self-limiting beliefs. This is not necessarily about others speaking positively in your life, but what YOU say to yourself that matters above all.

Confident Face

I am going to give *six* practical declarations, and I want you to speak them over your life every day. Say these declarations with conviction:

1) I am fearfully and wonderfully made by God!
2) I have what it takes to obtain flawless skin!
3) I am greater than my weaknesses because I overcome them with positive words!
4) I am not my spots, acne, discoloration, fears, hyperpigmentation or anxiety!
5) I will invest in the best skincare that suits my skin type and needs!
6) I am determined to build up on self-confidence and invest in personal development!

When you say these declarations with power, you are owning who you are and fear eventually subsides. Do not wait for anyone to approve of you. When you look within yourself, take the time to remove all the distractions and *keep focused.* When I thought about the title of this book, I remembered the times I didn't feel confident in sharing my skin journey.

Although it was obvious that I had severe breakouts, I had to look within myself and ask whether I was ready to share my story. I knew that I wasn't the only one who went through the stages of breakouts, and I now use my life as a testimony to encourage and empower others to love who they are.

What is it that God cannot do when it comes to looking after your skin? In the book of Esther, she was treated as royalty and was assigned maids to pamper her to see the King. In Esther 2:10, it expresses that before a woman was to visit the King, the woman had to complete twelve months of beauty treatments prescribed for six months with oil of myrrh, and six months with perfumes and cosmetics.

Even in the Bible, you see women looking after their skin, ensuring that their beauty treatments are essential. We must understand how beautiful we are and learn many lessons from the Bible, especially to do with working on our inner and outer beauty.

As you are going higher, it starts with self-reflection, honesty and time away from all distractions. There is a price to pay to reach the next dimension. Luke 12:48 reminds us that when much is given, much more is required. As you look within yourself, what do you see that requires much of you, and how willing are you to commit? When you've overcome seasons of depression and anxiety, you're required to assist and help others who were once in your situation.

We shouldn't become proud and assume 'we have arrived.' You never know what tomorrow holds, and when you've been given a large platform to inspire and influence, remember where you came from and how you started.

Work on your heart intently, because the only person that can deceive you is YOU. I remember studying Matthew 23:25-26 (NIV) where Jesus spoke about seven woes on the teachers of the law and the Pharisees. This is what it says: *"Woe to you, teachers of the law and Pharisees; you hypocrites! You clean the outside of the cup and dish, but inside they are full of greed and self-indulgence. (26) Blind Pharisee! First clean the inside of the cup and dish, and then the outside also will be clean."*

As I studied this text, I understood the concept that Christ was expressing. At times, we tend to focus more on our external beauty to ensure we are seen as 'goals', however, our character, attitude, and behaviour to certain situations are completely the opposite. We complain, murmur and wonder why we are in the same position.

To be called a hypocrite is not pleasant; Jesus got serious here, and it's important that we too, take our lives seriously. Rather than always investing the majority of your time on how you look, when was the last time you had self-reflection and analysed your heart? If you are not happy with the status of your skin, what are you doing about it right now? It feels easy and comfortable to accept your skin for what it is, remaining complacent and not wanting to do anything about it.

You can do so much with your flaws, if you clean your heart and use gentle words soothing to the soul. We should never underestimate the power of Proverbs 16:24 which says – *"Pleasant words are like a honeycomb, sweetness to the soul and health to the bones."*

It's the words that shape and make you who you are. Your words shouldn't make you speak what you feel; instead, take control over your emotions and change the way you internalise thoughts. In Chapter 3 of The Power of a Forward-Thinking Mindset, I entitled it *'focused and firm.'* Most times in our lives we can be triggered by what we hear and see. I understand that each day will have its own challenges, however, I am disciplined in how much attention I give to it, for what you focus on will magnify.

When you don't have the time to reflect on your own life and use other external resources as a means to 'try and forget' what's in front of you, it makes it difficult to be free. Don't put yourself in danger because of dysfunction. Having countless thoughts is not for you to indulge in.

Give it to the One that knows the number of hairs on your head (Luke 12:7.) When we lay aside every weight that easily entangles us, and makes us feel we need to control every aspect of our lives, that is where peace starts to come in.

We can't assume that our methods will always be right. No number of products, masks, creams, or tablets can suffice. I've tried everything, and once I gave my struggles to the Lord, my life hasn't been the same. Of course, it's not always easy to surrender, especially when you are used to creating solutions on your own.

In essence, no matter how many books you read on getting the perfect skin, it will never be 100% perfect. Why? Because we live in an imperfect world. Being confident comes through Christ Jesus and His Word to mankind. I was always trying to find ways of making my skin work the way I'd wanted it to be, but ended up draining me because I didn't identify with the One who not only created me, but made me in His own image.

When we have to take responsibility for our own actions and face up to what we've done, it brings nerves and great tension, however, if you don't apply how to do this in the early stages of your life, you'll always be hiding from your troubles.

No matter where you are, always be accountable to your actions and learn from your mistakes. There will be seasons in your life where God will require the stillness within and not be distracted by external noises.

You don't have to make your life become what it needs to be; let it do what it's doing authentically. The more you keep tampering with your issues *without* the wise counsel of God, the outcome will result with reaping in your own strength. God's strength is made perfect in our weaknesses (2 Cor. 12:9) and being in the Presence of God enables Him to show you the flaws, brokenness and insecurities He wants to heal within you.

***

IMPORTANT: In order to heal the collective, you must heal within.

***

What is the purpose of helping everyone around you and feeling drained afterwards? That is a lot of baggage that needs to be cut off. The next step is to face your own giants and insecurities. The greater you face them, the easier it becomes to manage. We also must be aware that putting our dependency on others can trigger our self-esteem.

The Power of a Forward-Thinking Mindset focuses on the importance of being strong-minded in adversity, whilst being determined to move ahead. When you can stand firm and remain focused on what is ahead of you, it opens the right opportunities and cultivates healthy relationships. This does not only impact those around us, but our minds and physical health adapts to how we think and eventually produces healthy thoughts. If our thoughts are in alignment with what we believe ourselves to be, it becomes easier to manage and understand life from a healthy perspective.

It can become easier to focus on the negative aspects in our lives which cause us to become dysfunctional and fruitless. When was the last time you were silent and focused attentively on your own thoughts? It is important to have time for yourself and listen to the way you've been feeding your thoughts. It shouldn't always be someone else's responsibility if you don't learn how to be accountable for your own journey.

When you upgrade your mind, you upgrade your life. You don't always have to be consumed with what you hear. There are times where people speak into your life, but they don't need to speak into your spirit. It is your spirit that enables you to reject what isn't yours without letting the words shape who you are.

The words that go into your ears can't compare to what goes in your spirit. There is a difference – it takes time to let go of words, especially if they have cut deep, therefore, be intentional about the words you keep and the words you must disregard.

I'll ask you today: What lens are you using to look at your situation? Ask yourself why it's comfortable to remain the same. *Don't be a burden to your environment; add value to it*. We don't need to see another version of our insecurities. Whether you want to believe it or not, those you admire have their flaws too. You ought to be inspired by them, but not to imitate them. Learn from their lessons and apply it to your own personal journey in skin and health care.

If you don't take the time to look within yourself, analyse and reflect on your thoughts, you will succumb to what someone else wants you to be. Giving another person the authority to speak over your life will take a certain level of *access*. How much access are you willing to give out? Let it be done in wisdom and confide in God more than your feelings.

***

IMPORTANT: You give your feelings power when you don't spend quality time in the *Secret Place*.

***

When it comes to your future, how you see yourself at this present time will determine how tomorrow will look. This is why Matthew 6:34 will forever be one of my favourite messages. Each day has its own troubles of its own, so <u>focus on one day at a time</u>. If you look towards the future with the eyes of fear, you will eventually underestimate the power of God. When you underestimate the One that created you in His image, you underestimate your own beauty. You can't re-create yourself, neither can you steal someone else's gifts and talents.

When there is pressure to use what others are promoting, have you considered whether it will end up working for or against you? Have you taken the time to understand and know your skin inside out? Have you learnt to love and embrace who you are despite what other people say? Galatians 1:10 speaks about not living for the audience of many, but of One. Do not settle on what you hear or see; be confident in who you are within.

If you want great blessings, you need to think great thoughts and take action. Your thoughts attract the blessings. Your words bring them into manifestation. Your actions will ultimately lead to the results. There is no time to settle for less when God has made you to be the best!

Let this sink in: If you want clear skin, look within. If you want a better life, look within. If you want to build on your own confidence, look within. All these values are already in you. It takes a strong-minded individual to believe it, even when it looks impossible. We don't always want to take responsibility for how we feel, but that is the way we can identify and work on our character.

Having everything at once is dangerous and unhealthy. There are lessons to learn in the process of healing, and I had to take every lesson on board when going through my skincare journey. What did the process teach me? Patience. Self-love. Kindness.

If everything goes the way you planned, would your character remain the same, or would there be the temptation to become proud? It's in the vulnerable moments that we gain strength, become wiser and know what we must value.

When you are alone in your room, you need to make time and have a 'heart-to-heart' conversation with yourself. Grab a chair, sit back and talk with yourself. *Ask*: 'Am I a good person to be around?' When you can answer that question in honesty, you will be able to identify whether you add value or you are a liability.

In chapter 2, I spoke about distinguishing assets from liabilities, which I highly recommend you to read again as a reminder. When you know who you are, you'll know the value you bring to the table. There is only so much one can do, and when it becomes unbearable, we start looking for approval elsewhere.

It's in the stillness that you are able to work thoroughly within; it silences your emotions and restless thoughts that cause you to make decisions in haste. Making decisions too quickly prevents you from looking within. The less control you have over your life, the stronger you become in depending on God more.

***

IMPORTANT: Facing your giants will require you to face yourself first!

***

In order to be effective in your own lane, you must learn how to focus on one area at a time. Looking within will require maturity. It isn't about having life go your own way, but learning from the mistakes of the past, and using them to push you forward. This is not the time to be complacent but to look within and ask those *hard questions*. It's time to change your mindset. Fight them on your knees and you will win!

8

○

Yes, water and minding your own business helps!

You can achieve far more when you are F.O.C.U.S.E.D!

I cannot emphasise on the word F.O.C.U.S enough! In as much as it's important to help and encourage people from time to time, there will be moments where you need to take yourself out of an individual's situation and focus on your own journey. You can't carry everyone's burdens; it will be too much for you to handle.

I remember talking to a dear friend about this topic and what occurred to me was that, every time an opportunity appeared to help someone, it was a great way to encourage the individual, but other times, I had to allow the person to make decisions for themselves.

If not, they can make you feel like you are some type of *god* – in other words, we idolise people because we feel they relate and understand us – this is dangerous and there should be a healthy limit to how much we can do for people. *Be firm in saying no if you aren't led to help*. Don't give yourself more work, on top of the challenges that are happening in your life too.

Confident Face

At times, there is a tendency to build ones' confidence based on their skin issues, but realise that, until they are willing to do the work, they can't be helped. There are more practical ways of helping your skin flourish throughout all seasons; winter, spring, summer and fall. The impact water has on our skin makes a great difference and also helps the body to flush out waste.

According to skinkraft.com website, it states that drinking ample water balances the oil and content on the skin, which helps to prevent excess oil and sebum secretion, resulting in fewer clogged pores and acne. Adult acne, on the other hand, is becoming more common due to change of lifestyles and lack of hydration. Four to six people out of 100 in the age groups of 20 to 40 have adult acne. Source: **www.skinkraft.com**.

As you grow older, your skin becomes prone to acne breakouts, because of the changes in eating habits, thoughts and the environment. When it comes to washing your face, however, gentle care must be applied to it using lukewarm water (not hot or cold). When you want to see changes in your skin, you have to put in the consistent effort. It may not seem obvious all the time, because it's a natural tendency to help others in their time of need.

Confident Face

There was a time where my skin broke out drastically between the months of July-September 2019. During my third book launch in July 2019, my face was extremely spotty. I initially booked an MUA to do my make-up for the launch but decided not to proceed.

Alternatively, I used YouTube to find tips on how to hide spots and blackheads which I endeavoured to apply concealer over them. When I arrived at the book launch, I was visualising in my mind that someone would ask what happened with my skin. To my surprise, nobody asked; it kept me silent for a while. I believe it was my calm aura that made no one ask, as I didn't allow my emotions to control my thoughts, or, perhaps, they knew and didn't want to ask for respect purposes.

What I've learnt during the process of getting clear skin is that, when you see someone that has breakouts, do not stare too much! You don't know how they're feeling, and if you don't have anything nice to say, do not say anything at all. I give full attention to not only minding your own business, but looking at your heart and intentions.

If we are not careful, we can think we're doing someone a favour, but it's hit that sensitive place and sparked more spots and breakouts. Even when you see someone that isn't confident in who they are, rather than asking them multiple questions, allow them to express themselves first. Don't put words into their mouth if they aren't ready to speak. Give everyone *their own time*.

We must get to a place in our lives where the cry of another person doesn't cause us to become nosey, leading us to bleed and feel sorry for them, rather, allowing them to take responsibility for who they are. You will save a lot of heartache by being silent and offer encouraging words as an alternative.

I came across 1 Thessalonians 4:11 which expresses five factors I believe reflects on minding your own affairs and living a productive life. Let's take a look at the following:

1) **To lead and live a quiet life** – a life that is led in humility is a life worth praising. Do not lead a flamboyant lifestyle that requires everyone to know all about you. You must put a price tag on who you are and learn to build in silence. Let the final outcome be what inspires others to be influenced, not only by your humility, but the silent seasons you're in, that is building you to be the best version of yourself. Remember, silence is confidence. Don't allow anyone to make you speak prematurely or talk without wisdom.

2) **To mind your own business** – we must cultivate this attitude to mind our own business until we are informed about a situation. It is better to be invited in a discussion or involved in an activity, rather than being boastful and assume you are among the community, for a senior spokesperson to inform you to go to the back of the room. Proverbs 25:7 (NLT) puts it like this: "It is better to wait for an invitation to the head table than to be sent away in public disgrace."

3) **To work with your hands** – Proverbs 18:16 (NIV) says "A gift opens the way and ushers the giver into the presence of the great." What is in your hand is greater than what someone else can offer you. If you doubt what's in your hands i.e. the gifts and talents you have, you will always be at the detriment of other people's expectations.

4) **To influence outsiders** – it's better to be an influencer than to allow others to influence you. The more you are able to inspire and impact those around you, the easier it becomes to build upon your own self-confidence and limit the external noises. There are those who have the gift of influencing and attracting crowds that don't look like them, however, it's

important to stay true to yourself and know who you are.

5) **To depend on nobody** – when it comes to dependence, this is not to say that we can't depend on anyone at all, but there must be *wisdom* applied when we confide in others. It is not healthy to depend on people all the time; however, you must get to a stage where you make decisions without the consent or approval of others. There will be people who are strong advocates and assets where you can be open with, depending on the nature of the relationship and the trust built. Remember, not everyone has the right to speak into your life, so keep your ears and discernment levels sharp.

Applying the above factors in your life will save you from failed friendships and relationships. To add on this, when you come to a place where you desire real change, it will take a lot of humility. I believe living a quiet life is important, to not interfere with other people's affairs and keep your focus ahead to avoid being in trouble.

When it comes to using what you have, how intentional are you to work with it? For example, the skincare product that irritates your skin; what are you doing about it?

Confident Face

Are you still using those products because you spent a lot of money on it? Disregard any product that isn't doing your skin the good it needs, and be confident in what you are already using. Remember to speak positively over your face, your skin and your products.

Above all, when you know that looking in the mirror is your 1-2-1 reflection, that is when your confidence becomes stronger and you learn how to depend on God more. I've had to fight my way in tears, in prayer, in fasting and being away from distractions to see changes in my skin. I understand that it's no-one else's responsibility to be accountable and work on the changes that I desire to see. The same applies to you as well!

Minding your own business is a healthy contributing factor in one's life; depending on the level of your understanding and maturity levels, it has a very important element to it and will help in the long term to build trust with people and opportunities. Not everything has to be shared at once, and as I say from time to time: *'silence is confidence!'* When you aren't required to talk, you are in the right place to meditate and reflect.

Before you speak, ask yourself whether what will come out of your mouth will add value or crush the person's spirit. Some people are emotionally bruised;

being a person that is on their journey of self-discovery and freedom may not require you to speak, but instead, listen attentively to what the person is saying. It may take time to heal, whilst others have developed and worked on their maturity levels.

Do you find it difficult focusing, that your itching ears want to know everything? When you focus on your own lane, you have the time, energy and patience to work on yourself, whilst having a consistent skincare routine. When your focus is divided, it becomes difficult to hear your own voice.

At times, you may end up comparing your skincare journey to another and may cause you to become unaware that they also had skin issues at the initial stages. However, I don't only want to emphasise on minding your own business from a practical or skincare perspective; I also want you to focus on your spiritual walk and relationship with God.

The two most intense seasons for my skin was in my second year of university and during the summer period of 2019. I was frustrated that my skin wasn't working the way I'd expected it to, and it was a struggle talking about it to my friends.

I didn't take the time to leave all the emotional concern in God's Hands. Instead, I chose to invest in other products that were advertised online and took matters into my own hands. I was being nosey in God's great work and didn't have the patience to wait on Him to come through.

In a fast-paced society that encourages instant gratification, it's easy to desire quick-fix results, but we should never expect to see our Father in that light. Everything He does is perfect and on time. We ought to give Him room to make decisions on our behalf, knowing that He will deliver.

I understand what it feels like for the young insecure woman to secretly compare herself with others. Looking great on social media, but behind closed doors, crying each night, asking when the mental instability will end. When I took my focus off my condition, my relationship with God became more intimate, and I started seeing changes in my life. I had to let go of being in control and minding my own affairs by being in His Presence without any interruptions.

It's not to say that you have to be fully focused on yourself and not consider others around you, but there is a time and season for everything under the sun; a time to socialise, a time to be alone, a time to help and a time to mind your own affairs. The key is *balance*.

Confident Face

In a world that becomes consumed with self, distractions crop up. How do you respond to noise? Why is it easy to be involved in other people's lives, yet fail to invest in your own personal development? We wait for people to approve and make us feel good, not realising that they can praise you today and criticise you tomorrow! I've learnt the importance of working consistently on my character which is an on-going process.

When you wake up in the morning, who is the first person on your mind? A confident individual is eager to improve and enhance themselves to make their environment better. However, they must first identify where their strengths and weaknesses are and distinguish the root of them in a healthy manner. An individual that takes the time to work on their weaknesses and build on their strengths is focused and determined to succeed.

Jealousy and envy, on the other hand, are easy iniquities to slip into. It's easy to look around at what others have and feel that your life ought to be different. What someone is jealous for may be a strong attainment they feel they've worked for, i.e. a prize, recognition for hard work, or better circumstances. Instead, a lifestyle of contentment is important to have in order to prevent toxic thoughts.

A person of integrity and confidence doesn't entertain jealousy. Yes, we are human, but that doesn't grant the right to entertain those thoughts and assume you should have more than the other person. In essence, you could be envious that your friend has beautiful skin, but misunderstand that they had to work on their inner being to have healthy skin.

Question: Have you prayed about the situation? Have you spoken to God about how you feel and surrendered it to Him? Everyone is on their own healing journey and there is only so much you can do to help, however, when it's time to let go of the wheel and trust God who is in charge, you will start to see your life from a clearer perspective.

As long as you allow God to do what only He can, you will always feel the need to take the battle in your own hands. In essence, when we become our own self-made individuals, we entertain *secret pride*. We certainly need saving from ourselves, because so often, we think we know best, reaching for self-dependence. We set up and follow paths of our own choosing only to find that some paths lead to destruction and long-term personal digging. When this happens, this is where you need to admit where you went wrong and give God room to move.

I understand the feeling when we assume our decisions are always right; why not? It sounds right in the ears; our emotions and feelings confirm it as well. However, feelings can't always be trusted. You can be happy today and tomorrow, something attempts to trigger you.

In 2020, I learnt the importance of *giving God room and time.* I've taken my thoughts and suggestions out and surrendered them as 1 Peter 5:7 encourages us to, allowing Him to do the best work. I encourage you to give Him room and rest in His promises.

***

IMPORTANT: In order to see change, learn to mind your affairs and work on yourself.

***

"It's such a beautiful feeling when you know what you've been called to do without entertaining any form of inadequacy. Build your own craft and work on your current skill set and see it work in your favour. You are your own brand! Remember that!"

Everyone has a unique gift, calling, talent and skill. If you allow what someone else is doing to deter you from focusing, you will be side-tracked. No two fingers are the same. Remember this and you will be ready for life. When it comes to minding your own affairs, it takes consistent strength. It won't always be convenient for others, but you must ensure that it's convenient for you.

You should surround yourself with the right people who remind you to focus on what's in front of you. Everything in life is constantly changing – this is inevitable. Be intentional about your own change, be true to your authentic calling and let confidence blossom, despite the pressure and second-guesses. You have what it takes to be the best in your field. *Yes, you need the right people, but in order to have the right people, you must work on being the right person.*

You must learn how to enjoy your own company in different seasons; where you are right now is not the definition of your life. You are going higher, whether you don't see or feel anything happening right now. With time, you will understand. It takes strength to do the work, but it has to be done. Focusing on your own journey will help you understand who you are and what you've been called to do.

For the purpose of peace, ease and maturity, it's not all situations you have to be involved in. There are some circumstances that will not require you not to speak or share opinions for your own benefit. Being led and seeking wisdom are wise steps to take before contributing to a statement that may trigger someone.

Confident Face

No one is expecting you to drain yourself out at the expense of another person's mental well-being, however, it's important to know when to mind your own business and when to speak.

When it comes to building confidence, it is a long-term investment. Working on your emotional stability, building your mental state, surrounding yourself with those who have more knowledge and expertise, and physically working on your health, are key ways to focus on becoming a better individual.

In order to see change, you need to adopt a *growth mindset* where you are capable of learning new skills and abilities. A *fixed mindset* can cause you to stick with the regular routines and miss out on opportunities. I remember many times where I'd gave several matters to the Lord, to find out that I took it back and became my own 'Bob the Builder.' I realised that every time I got in the Lord's way, it delayed the process. I was concerned about the timing and when my desires would come to fruition.

The feeling of being in control can leave you drained. LEAVE IT AT THE ALTAR! If you need to keep hearing this so you can let go, it is worth it. Focus on what's in front of you because this will enable the Lord to do His great work in you.

Confident Face

You don't always need to know what your future will look like because the future is filled with expensive gifts money cannot buy. When you are confident in the One that knows you personally, it will encourage you to let go of your agenda, trying to make yourself look complete and have it all together, when you know that it's not always going to be the case.

Not having everything go your way can be a blessing. I didn't realise this until I learnt to mind my own business and let God do His work. The joy we desire to have is when we submit and surrender everything.

Emotions will eventually start warning you of how to act, what to say and how to feel. Making a permanent decision based on a temporary situation is not healthy. Admit and let out the tears if you have to for it cleanses the soul, however, don't allow it to deter you or cause you to act out of pity and low self-esteem. *Focus* requires self-discipline and minding your own affairs that require you to submit.

Be careful of people who portray a form of confidence, and are deeply and secretly insecure because of your own confidence. It's not enough to pretend to be confident; you need to thoroughly examine and work on your inner being and find out what's causing you to act in uncertain and controlling ways. Don't bring down someone's organic confidence because you choose not to take responsibility for your own lack of confidence.

Learn to work on your heart and thoughts and ensure that your words are free from corrupt talk and perversity (*Proverbs 4:24*). You will save a lot of time being someone you are not, and eventually attract the right people who will love the REAL YOU! You have confidence already embedded in you; stop making others want to praise your cracked ego. It's not healthy and will affect others around you if not dealt with on time. Mind your own affairs and work on YOU!

9

o

Confident Face

***Confidence is not bringing people down. Confidence is
being able to inspire and transform the minds of others in
your environment that don't see anything good about
themselves.***

He *remained silent for a while, and that caused me to seek
Him even more* – an excerpt from Bishop TD Jakes Book
Crushing. When it comes to confidence, it's not in your
power to think you have it all together. Confidence is in the
One who created and made you in His likeness. We must not
forget that when we achieve greatness, it started with God
having us in mind, and granting us the ability and gifts to be
fruitful and multiply.

What does *fruit* look like? I am not referring to the fruit we
eat on a daily basis, but the work we put into our daily lives
in order to reap a harvest, which includes spiritual maturity,
self-control and peace of mind. Having a confident face takes
focus, determination and consistency. Confidence can feel
like a long process, especially when you are preparing to
launch a new product or service.

Confident Face

You would've done thorough research about your target market, the purpose behind your new venture, and ultimately, the solution that your products or services aim to provide to your customers. However, being able to understand the beauty of patience, humility and perseverance will also take time when building a brand or business from scratch.

Confidence starts with a prayer before it becomes a reality. Speak to the Father regarding what's on your heart, no matter how big or small it may be. It is important to honour your emotions and surrender them to the One that knows how to handle them. Let's take a look at the following points of being a confident face:

Being a confident face means you overcome uncertainty and the barriers that try to limit you.

Being a confident face is when you are able to triumph over situations that you couldn't handle in your own strength.

Moreover, being confident is when you are able to come boldly to the throne of Grace knowing that the help you need is already in your reach (Heb 4:16.) When you don't feel good enough or reminded of how your skin made you feel in the past, remember how far God's taken you; look back and *thank your pain.*

Confident Face

There will be moments in our lives where fear speaks louder. When we have been called to influence, inspire and build legacies, fears of the past and the unknown future robs us of our current destiny. Other times, the issues of life start streaming down and it becomes too much to handle.

Remember to not only have the form of a confident face, but *be* the confident individual wherever you go. Not only in your make-up, but in the character that reflects your words and actions. Living in a society where everyone is imitating each other becomes competitive, repetitive and boring. There needs to be a difference that causes others to wonder how you keep going.

As I had the vision to talk about my skincare journey, I had the opportunity of asking two women to share their experiences with their skin and how they overcame their breakouts. Through their transparency, I want you to be encouraged. What your skin is going through has an expiry date. Read their stories:

Confident Face

My story with Melvina E:

I've always done the facial wash and exfoliating routine for many years, but it was not a consistent routine. Sometimes, I would fall asleep without washing my face after a day out. I might just lazily wipe my face with baby wipes and doze off. My skin reflected on the lack of effort and attention I was giving to it. It would break out into angry spots; ironically it would be around a special occasion or the day I needed my skin to co-operate.

Is a flawless skin too much to ask for? I always knew that my expectations of a blemish-free and flawless skin required time and effort on my part. I needed to love this temple the best way possible and show it the gentle love and care that it yearned for, but time, I did not have. Long hours at work, constantly feeling tired and the idea that other things were of a higher priority, thus requiring more of my time. So, I carried on with my inconsistent and hurried skin care "routine."

Then, the pandemic called "coronavirus" happened. We were forced into lockdown. The world stopped and time stopped. I was forced to stop in my heels and put things into perspective. The time which I always felt I needed more of had been given to me in abundance. Ample time to reflect on my past actions. Nowhere to go; just me, myself and I.

Confident Face

I focused on my temple that God gave me and started with my skin. I tried out different products and was shocked that I hadn't started this earlier. Natural products that our Father has blessed this world with and has given us the wisdom to mix concoctions and recipes to enhance our bodies with.

I was amazed and full of awe about the science behind our bodies inside and out. I realised that my skin responded well to black soap; it loved the vapour of my steam machine, and rejoiced when I massaged my whipped shea butter infused with essential oils into my skin. And so, my skin glowed; it felt supple and young. I did not need to lather my face in makeup all the time. I let my skin speak for itself.

The confidence and joy it gave me reminded me that I reap whatever I sow and my skin was bearing fruits from the labour of my consistent skin care routine. Persistence, patience, effort and consistency led to the confidence I felt in my new skin. For once I could meet my friends without feeling like I had to bathe my face in makeup.

With this, I'll urge everyone to adopt a skin care routine, find the time to understand your skin, understand what it likes and does not like. Be patient with it, for Rome was not built in a day. Feed it the nutrients that it needs to flourish and watch it glow in return.

Confident Face

We have one life to live and one skin to live in. How we treat it now will determine how we look in 20 years' time. Let's be kind to our skin. Be kind to you!

Confident Face

My story with Wendy Odili:

The skin care journey is one that comes with a lot of ups and downs. It is difficult to feel like your shine is being hindered. You get tempted to feel down and defeated and the challenge with having battles with your skin is often greatly misunderstood. It is an enemy that attempts to steal your peace, your confidence, your beauty and oh goodness, your money!

As you embark on much trial and error with different types of products and treatments in your war against these skin issues, and in your bid and sincere desperate desire to get that perfect healthy and glowing skin that you deserve. But as you go through it, you must always remember no matter what battles you face with your skin, know that your beauty is not defined by them.

Underneath those scars, those pimples is a glowing Queen; and the truth is that true beauty radiates from within and is defined from that inner place of a quiet and gentle spirit. The battle is temporary, the challenges are not unbeatable. Even if the journey is slow and painful, which it normally is, and it does require much patience, you will be undefeated; you will indeed win over this enemy and you will radiate all your glory and beauty as you should. You are still beautiful and no skin care issue can take that away.

Confident Face

As I was reading Melvina and Wendy's stories, I resonated with them in many ways, particularly, when Melvina spoke about utilising natural products, and taking the time to build consistently in her skincare routine. Wendy transparently spoke about her pimples and how they didn't define her. This reminds me of beauty that already starts from within.

My vision for this book is to consistently remind readers that they are not defined by the breakouts on their skin or their flaws and insecurities. It takes a lot of strength for people to be free and express themselves in a way that is open to vulnerability, and even, criticism.

It's in the weak positions that healing begins, and this book project wouldn't have been written if there wasn't a time in my life where I broke out. To the many men and women who are growing up to become great leaders in the future, let this book continue to encourage and elevate you to achieve more.

Work on yourself, work on your character; be firm in who you are and learn to own your confidence. Giving others the ability to define who you are or allowing society to control you is too expensive.

A word of encouragement: you are more than your bruises, scars and burns. We've had our fair share of insecurities, but NOW is the time to put on your confident face and embrace your authentic beauty. NOW is the time to rise above unreliable emotions and feelings of what the past labelled you to be. You are more than what you consume. Believe it. Accept it, and remember what God says about you. Real confidence comes from the One that knows you by name. As long as you remember who you are, confidence will walk with you in every journey of life.

We must come out of the lies we tell ourselves, especially in a world where it creates a false perception of happiness. This is not healthy and doesn't bring about the wholeness that is needed to be a confident individual. You have to be intentional about how you think, and ultimately what you speak into your life.

If we are not careful, we will make excuses not to change, and blame it on the past, our loved ones, our friends, the society and refuse to look within and take responsibility. Ultimately, remember that not everyone is for you; therefore, do not change to be what others want you to be. Be who God has called you to be.

When the time is right for a choice to be made in your own environment, you will know, and I will assist you through it. Until that time, be sure that merely keeping close to Me guarantees you are moving in the right direction, despite questions and doubt raging in your mind, and ultimately building your own confidence in Me who made you perfectly.

Confident Face

The sooner we learn to accept God as He is, not as we would like Him to be, the sooner we will move from the path of confusion to confidence.

If you feel a gap or numbness when people around you are being blessed or walking in their purpose, you may have to revisit your relationship life with God and ask Him to fill you with His full attention that you forget your own feelings and rest in His own promises for your life. It's all about relationship-building with Jesus. That's how you overcome self-limiting beliefs and ultimately build your own confident face. But, remember to build *with* Him. Remember to stay integral. You must be yourself. You can't duplicate the original.

Hebrews 10:35-36 says: *"So do not throw away your **confidence**; for it will be richly rewarded. You need to persevere so that when you have done the will of God, you will receive what he has promised."*

Even when the results don't show up when you expected it to, keep pushing. The more we keep seeking, the more answers we will receive, but it depends on how patient we are to wait for the ultimate results. It takes great grace and patience to wait and be expectant to get an answer. Confidence is not always having everything go your way.

Confident Face

You can still be confident in rejection because it is ultimately redirecting you on the right path. You'll have to learn how to embrace unexpected changes in your life that come up and keep it moving.

Confidence is being able to work with what you have left, even if along the way there have been valuables that have been lost or misplaced. If everything you planned went your way, you would be very happy right? But, have you ever considered why your deadlines and God's deadlines aren't the same? This is the reason why we ought to build our confidence in Him and not in our timelines. The process in getting to the next destination is in the *waiting*.

I remember giving a dear friend a proverb to study and ponder on. It was Proverbs 3:5-6, but the main verse I put emphasis on was verse 6 which says "***acknowledge*** Him in all your ways in He shall direct your paths." The word *acknowledge* is appreciating and welcoming an individual's presence, honouring and noticing them. It's a great feeling when you are appreciated!

Acknowledgement is a gift and sign of trust and confidence. When someone can trust you with a secret, you will cherish that person because they see you as reliable and trustworthy. A confident individual has the ability to believe what that person says and will be true to their word (integrity.) This is the same with God. He wants us to build our confidence in Him and our identity. When you honour Him with your time, efforts and lifestyle, He will show you the ways to go and you will know it because peace is attached to it.

Confidence and peace are both attractive. Analyse your heart and your thoughts – why are you behaving a certain way that is causing you to act differently? Ultimately, take time out to reflect on what thoughts you're entertaining to see if they are healthy for you and your environment. Remember to be your own confident face and acknowledge the One that made you, beautifully and fearfully. If you haven't heard this in a while, remember that you are BEAUTIFUL!

"Your beauty should not come from outward adornment, such as elaborate hairstyles and the wearing of gold jewellery or fine clothes. Rather, it should be that of your inner self, the unfading beauty of a gentle and quiet spirit, which is of great worth in God's sight."

1 Peter 3:3-4.

Confident Face

Testimonials

Testimonials grant visitors and readers the opportunity for others to know the value and impact books make in society. This is what helps Authentic Worth publish more books, support aspiring authors and create a wide community of writers that will publicise their work and change lives. Authentic Worth Publishing would appreciate leaving a review on *Confident Face*. Your feedback is appreciated and will help us continue the journey of storytelling and book writing. Please leave your review(s) on our website here: **www.authenticworth.com/books**. Many thanks in advance.

References

All Recipes – What is the Daniel Fast?:
https://www.allrecipes.com/article/what-is-the-daniel-fast/

American Academy of Dermatology Association:
https://www.aad.org/public/parents-kids/healthy-
habits/parents/kids/skin-layers

Benefits of Salt Water for Skin Blog (Feb 2020):
https://www.mydcsi.com/2020/02/25/benefits-salt-water-
for-skin/

Dermnetnz.org:
https://dermnetnz.org/topics/nodulocystic-acne/

Eucerin (5 components that our skin protects us from):
https://int.eucerin.com/about-skin/basic-skin-
knowledge/skins-protective-barrier

Healthline.com:
https://www.healthline.com/health/beauty-skin-
care/cystic-acne

Mayo Clinic: https://www.mayoclinic.org/healthy-lifestyle/adult-health/expert-answers/healthy-skin/faq-20058184

Newsinhealth.nih.gov: https://newsinhealth.nih.gov/2015/11/keep-your-skin-healthy

Skinkraft.com: https://skinkraft.com/blogs/articles/benefits-of-drinking-water-for-skin

Tatcha.com: https://www.tatcha.com/blog/How-to-determine-your-skin-type.html

Lightning Source UK Ltd.
Milton Keynes UK
UKHW012006070621
385112UK00001B/197